Made in the USA
Monee, IL
22 March 2022

93373749R00057